VOLCANOES

BY SALLY M. WALKER

LERNER PUBLICATIONS COMPANY • MINNEAPOLIS

The photographs in this book are used with the permission of: Austin Post/U.S. Geological Survey, pp. 1, 6 (background), 14 (background), 24 (background), 32 (background), 36 (background), 39, 44–47 (background); © Art Wolfe/The Image Bank/Getty Images, p. 1 (title type); © Brad Lewis/Visuals Unlimited, p. 4; © Amos Nachoum/CORBIS, p. 5; © Tarko Sudiarno/AFP/Getty Images, p. 6; © G. Brad Lewis/Science Faction /Getty Images, p. 7; © Alison Wright/Robert Harding World Imagery/Getty Images, p. 8; © Doug Perrine/SeaPics.com, p. 10; C. Stoughton/U.S. Geological Survey, p. 11; R. L. Christiansen /U.S. Geological Survey, p. 12; D. W. Peterson/U.S. Geological Survey, pp. 13, 48 (bottom); National Park Service, p. 14; © Adam Jones/Visuals Unlimited, p. 15; © Inga Spence/Visuals Unlimited, p. 17; © Altitude/Peter Arnold, Inc., p. 19; © Travel Pix/Taxi/Getty Images, p. 20; © Bill Curtsinger/National Geographic/Getty Images, p. 21; © Science VU/NURP/Visuals Unlimited, p. 22; D. A. Swanson/U.S. Geological Survey, pp. 24, 48 (top); © Roger Ressmeyer/CORBIS, p. 25; © Marli Miller/Visuals Unlimited, pp. 26, 40; © William Huber/Stone+/Getty Images, p. 27; U.S. Geological Survey, pp. 28, 37; © Gerald & Buff Corsi/Visuals Unlimited, p. 29; © Charles Rogers/Visuals Unlimited, p. 30; © Raymond K. Gehman/National Geographic/Getty Images, p. 31; © Layne Kennedy/CORBIS, p. 32; © Scientifica/Visuals Unlimited, p. 33; © Wally Eberhart/Visuals Unlimited, pp. 34, 35; © Digital Vision/Getty Images, pp. 36, 46; © Bay Ismoyo/AFP/Getty Images, p. 38; J. D. Griggs/U.S. Geological Survey, p. 41; © Ron and Patty Thomas/Taxi/Getty Images, p. 42; © David Roth/Taxi/Getty Images, p. 43; © Bruce Alexander/AFP/Getty Images, p. 47.

Front cover: © Sylvain Grandadam/Stone/Getty Images.
Front cover Title Type: © Art Wolfe/The Image Bank/Getty Images.
Back cover: © Reuters/CORBIS.

Illustrations on pp. 9, 16, 18, 23 by Laura Westlund, copyright © by Lerner Publishing Group, Inc.

Copyright © 2008 by Sally M. Walker

Lerner Publications Company
A division of Lerner Publishing Group, Inc.
241 First Avenue North
Minneapolis, MN 55401 U.S.A.

Website address: www.lernerbooks.com

Library of Congress Cataloging-in-Publication Data

Walker, Sally M.
     Volcanoes / by Sally M. Walker.
          p.   cm. — (Early bird earth science)
     Includes index.
     ISBN-13: 978–0–8225–6733–2 (lib. bdg. : alk. paper)
     1. Volcanoes—Juvenile literature. I. Title.
QE521.3.W349 2008
551.21—dc22   2007001948

Manufactured in the United States of America
1 2 3 4 5 6 – JR – 13 12 11 10 09 08

CONTENTS

BE A WORD DETECTIVE

Can you find these words as you read about volcanoes? Be
a detective and try to figure out what they mean. You can
turn to the glossary on page 46 for help.

ash

caldera

cinder cones

composite
 volcanoes

crater

crust

erupts

hot spots

lahar

lava

magma

magma
 chamber

mantle

plates

pyroclastic
 rocks

shield volcanoes

vent

volcanoes

CHAPTER 1
WHAT IS A VOLCANO?

Earth has many volcanoes. Some volcanoes are tall mountains. Some are huge holes in the ground. Others are hidden under the oceans.

Volcanoes are places where hot, melted rock comes out of the ground. Most rock is hard. But when rock gets very, very hot, it melts. Melted rock is soft. It flows slowly, like toothpaste being squeezed out of a tube.

Melted rock can be so hot that it glows yellow or red.

Deep inside Earth, it is very hot. Some of the rock inside Earth gets so hot that it melts. Melted rock that is inside Earth is called magma (MAG-muh). Magma has a small amount of gas mixed into it. The gas is mostly steam. Steam is the gas that forms when water boils.

Steam is coming out of this volcano.

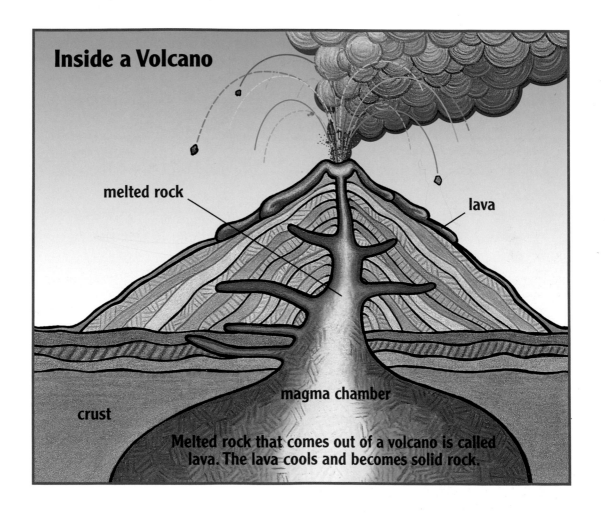

Inside a Volcano

melted rock

lava

crust

magma chamber

Melted rock that comes out of a volcano is called lava. The lava cools and becomes solid rock.

Magma moves around inside Earth. Hot magma weighs less than most solid rock. Because it is lighter, magma rises through cracks in solid rock. It fills up spaces in the rock. An underground space that is filled with magma is called a magma chamber.

9

Sometimes the magma pushes all the way to Earth's surface. Then the magma erupts. It spills out onto the surface. After magma flows onto the surface, it is called lava (LAH-vuh).

This volcano is under the Pacific Ocean. Red-hot lava is flowing across the ocean floor.

Lava is flowing from a vent inside this crater.

The opening from which lava flows is called a vent. A vent can be on a mountaintop. It can be on the side of a mountain. It can be on the ocean floor. Most vents are found inside craters. A crater is a hole shaped like a bowl.

Some lava is runny. Runny lava flows easily across the ground. Other lava is thicker. It spreads more slowly.

This lava is very thick.

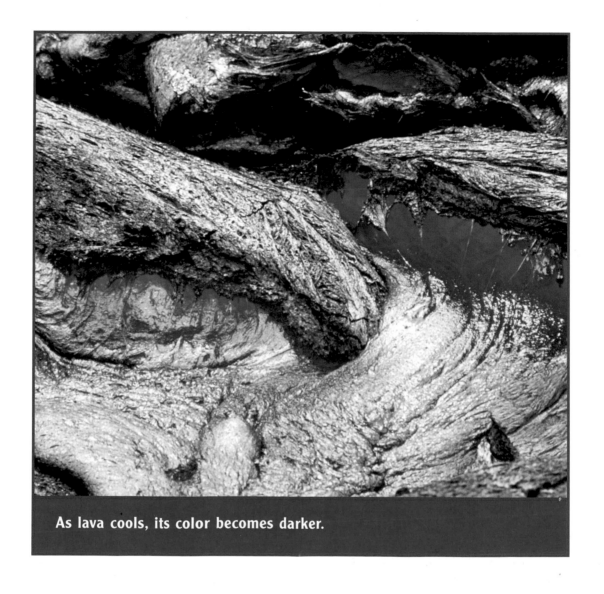
As lava cools, its color becomes darker.

When lava comes out of a volcano, it cools.
It changes into solid rock. Some lava rock has
a smooth surface. Other lava rock looks
chunky and rough.

In some places, part of Earth's rocky outer layer can be seen. What is this layer called?

CHAPTER 2

WHERE DO VOLCANOES FORM?

Earth has three main layers. The layers are the core, the mantle, and the crust. The core is

Earth's center. The mantle is Earth's thick middle layer. And the crust is Earth's outer layer. We live on Earth's crust.

Earth's crust is usually hidden under soil and plants.

The mantle is very hot. Rock melts in some areas of the mantle. The rock becomes magma.

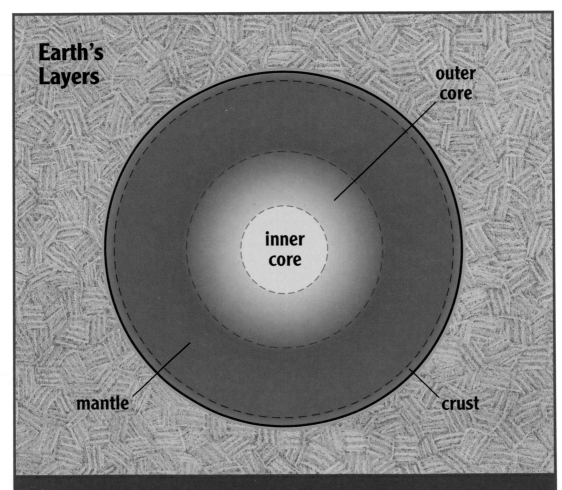

Earth's Layers

outer core

inner core

mantle

crust

Earth's three main layers are the core, the mantle, and the crust. Earth's core is divided into two parts. The inner core is solid, and the outer core is liquid. Scientists think most of the mantle is solid, but rock melts in some parts of it. The rock that makes up Earth's crust is solid.

Solid rock doesn't bend. If it is pushed hard enough, it breaks.

The crust is much cooler than the mantle.
Rock in the crust is solid. Solid rock cannot
bend and flow like magma.

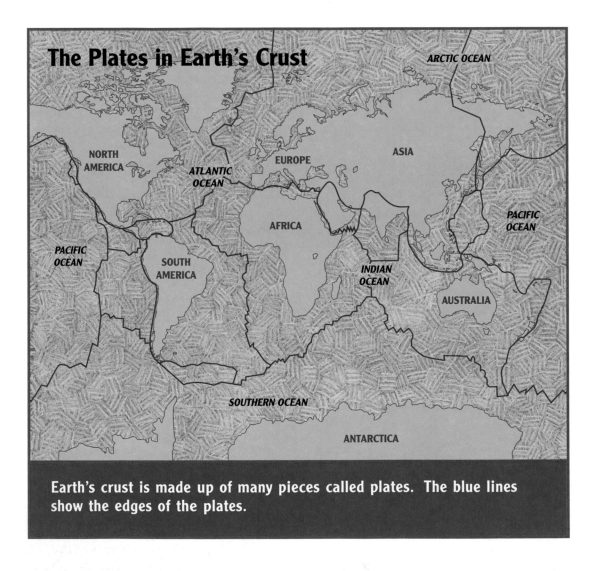

The Plates in Earth's Crust

ARCTIC OCEAN

NORTH AMERICA

EUROPE

ASIA

ATLANTIC OCEAN

PACIFIC OCEAN

PACIFIC OCEAN

AFRICA

SOUTH AMERICA

INDIAN OCEAN

AUSTRALIA

SOUTHERN OCEAN

ANTARCTICA

Earth's crust is made up of many pieces called plates. The blue lines show the edges of the plates.

Huge pieces of rock cover most of Earth's surface. They lie next to each other like the pieces of a puzzle. These pieces of rock are called plates. The top of each plate is made of rock from the crust. The bottom of the plate is made of rock from the top of the mantle. The plates slowly float on top of the rest of the mantle. In some places, plates push and slide against each other. In other places, plates pull away from each other.

The Great Rift Valley is in Africa. The valley formed because two of Earth's plates are slowly moving away from each other.

Most volcanoes form along the edges of the plates. When the plates push against each other or pull apart, rock gets squeezed or stretched. When the rock is squeezed or stretched, it gets hot. Some of it melts. It becomes magma. Wherever magma reaches the surface, a volcano forms.

Mount Fuji is a volcano in the country of Japan. Japan is near the edges of several of Earth's plates.

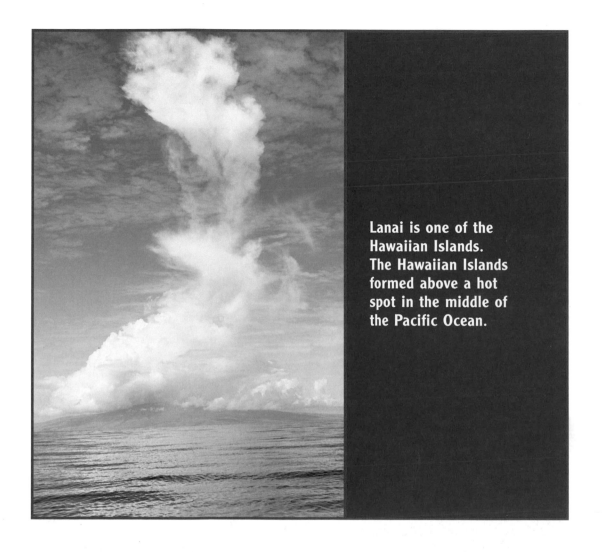

Lanai is one of the Hawaiian Islands. The Hawaiian Islands formed above a hot spot in the middle of the Pacific Ocean.

Volcanoes can also form far away from a plate's edges. Rock in some areas of the mantle gets extra hot. Scientists call these areas hot spots. In hot spots, magma pushes upward. It flows out of a vent and onto the surface.

The Hawaiian Islands are a chain of islands. They formed one by one above a hot spot in the Pacific Ocean. Magma erupted again and again into the water above the hot spot. The lava piled up higher and higher. After a long time, the lava rose above the water's surface. An island had formed. But the plate beneath it was moving the whole time.

Seawater quickly cools lava that erupts underwater. The lava hardens into big lumps.

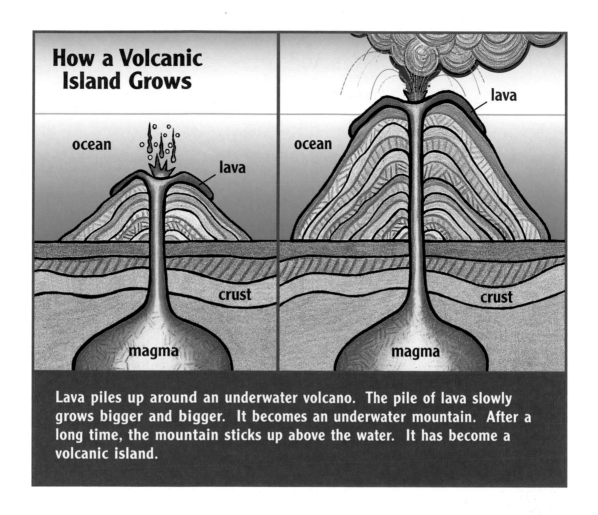

How a Volcanic Island Grows

ocean

lava

lava

ocean

crust

crust

magma

magma

Lava piles up around an underwater volcano. The pile of lava slowly grows bigger and bigger. It becomes an underwater mountain. After a long time, the mountain sticks up above the water. It has become a volcanic island.

Over many years, the plate carried the island away from the hot spot. Magma erupted from the hot spot again. A second island formed. Then that island was carried away from the hot spot. More and more islands formed as the plate kept moving.

This lava is runny. It is spreading out across the ground. What kind of volcano forms from runny lava?

CHAPTER 3
KINDS OF VOLCANOES

Some volcanoes have sides that are not very steep. These volcanoes look sort of like a fighter's shield lying on the ground. Scientists call them shield volcanoes.

Shield volcanoes form from lava that is runny, like syrup. Runny lava may flow for many miles before it cools and hardens. It covers the land like a huge blanket. Each time the volcano erupts, a new layer of lava is added on top of the old layers. As the layers pile up, they form a mountain that is shaped like a fighter's shield.

Mauna Kea is a shield volcano in Hawaii.

Some volcanoes are very tall, with steep sides. These volcanoes are called composite (kahm-PAH-ziht) volcanoes. They form from thick lava. Thick lava doesn't flow very far before it cools and hardens. More lava is added during later eruptions. The volcano becomes steeper and steeper. A tall, cone-shaped composite volcano forms.

Mount Hood is a composite volcano in the state of Oregon.

This cinder cone is in the country of New Zealand.

Cinder (SIHN-duhr) cones are small volcanoes with very steep sides. They form from magma that has a lot of gas bubbles in it. The bubbles explode when the magma flows out of a vent. Lava is thrown upward. It cools as it flies through the air. It becomes bits of solid rock. The rocks fall down around the vent. The pile of rock pieces gets taller each time the volcano erupts. After a while, the pile becomes a cinder cone.

These rocks are volcanic bombs.

Rocks thrown out of a volcano are called pyroclastic (PYE-roh-KLAS-tihk) rocks. Large pyroclastic rocks are called bombs. Bombs are the size of a baseball or larger. Other pyroclastic rocks are very small. They look like large grains of sand. These pyroclastic rocks are called ash. Big pyroclastic rocks fall to the ground like rain. Ash stays in the air longer. It can form huge clouds above a volcano.

Mount Saint Helens is a volcano in the state of Washington. Ash is coming out of its vent.

Sometimes very thick magma oozes from the vent in a volcano's crater. The lava piles up and becomes a lava dome. A lava dome looks like a tiny volcano inside a crater.

A lava dome is inside Mount Saint Helens's crater.

Crater Lake is a caldera in the state of Oregon. The caldera is filled with water from melting snow.

After a volcano erupts, part of the magma chamber under it is left empty. Sometimes the rock above the chamber is so heavy that it falls down. The rock falls into the empty magma chamber. It makes a hole called a caldera (kahl-DAIR-uh). A caldera is much larger than a crater.

Basalt (buh-SAHLT) is a kind of lava rock. What are some places where basalt is found?

CHAPTER 4
ROCKS FROM VOLCANOES

When lava comes out of a volcano, it cools and hardens. It becomes solid rock. Different kinds of lava become different kinds of rock.

One kind of lava rock is called basalt. The lava that erupts from volcanoes above hot spots usually hardens into basalt. The top of Earth's crust under the oceans is made of basalt.

Andesite (AN-dih-zyt) is another kind of lava rock. Andesite forms from thick magma. It often forms in places where one of Earth's plates slides under another plate.

Andesite was named after the Andes Mountains in South America.

Some magma is filled with many gas bubbles. The magma looks foamy. When foamy magma cools quickly, it becomes a kind of rock called pumice (PUH-muhs). Pumice is filled with tiny air bubbles. Air doesn't weigh much. The air inside pumice makes it weigh less than other kinds of rock. Pumice can be so light that it floats in water.

Pumice rock is full of holes.

Most obsidian rock is black.

Sometimes lava cools very quickly. Then it becomes a lava rock called obsidian (ahb-SIH-dee-uhn). Obsidian looks like dark glass. It is smooth and shiny. When it breaks, it has sharp edges.

Hot lava from a volcano set this house on fire. What is another way that volcanoes can be dangerous?

CHAPTER 5
VOLCANOES AND PEOPLE

Hot lava is dangerous. It can burn buildings. It can kill people and animals. But most lava flows slowly. People can usually see the lava coming and can get away from it.

Some volcanoes are much more dangerous than flowing lava. A big cloud of ash and rock may rush down the sides of a volcano. The cloud is called a pyroclastic flow. The flow is burning hot. It buries everything in its path. People cannot run fast enough to escape a pyroclastic flow. Many people may be killed.

Mount Saint Helens erupted in 1980. A cloud of ash and rock rushed down the side of the mountain.

Some volcanoes are tall mountains. Their tops are covered with snow and ice. When these volcanoes erupt, heat from magma melts the snow. The snow becomes water. The water runs down the mountain. As it flows, it mixes with soil and rocks to make mud. The flowing mud is called a lahar (LAH-hahr). The lahar gushes down the sides of the volcano. It knocks down trees, buildings, and huge rocks.

These houses were buried by rocks and sand that came from a volcano.

Some volcanoes make huge clouds of ash.

Wind can carry ash far from an erupting volcano. Some ash may be blown thousands of miles. Blowing ash is dangerous to airplanes. If a plane flies through an ash cloud, the ash gets sucked into the plane's engines. It makes the engines stop working. The plane may crash.

Volcanoes can change the weather too. Sunlight warms up the air. But a big ash cloud can block sunlight, the way rain clouds do. When ash blocks sunlight, Earth's air does not get as warm.

Rain clouds block sunlight. Ash from a volcano blocks sunlight too.

Earth's mantle is deep underground. Scientists can't look at it. To find out more about the mantle, scientists study lava from volcanoes. The lava started out as magma in Earth's mantle.

Scientists study volcanoes to find out if they might erupt. Sometimes the ground shakes near a volcano. It shakes because magma is moving far beneath the volcano. When the ground shakes a lot, the volcano may be about to erupt. Then scientists warn people who live nearby. They tell people to go to a safer place.

Volcanoes can be dangerous. But they can also help people. Over time, lava rocks break apart. The pieces of rock become part of the soil. Plants grow very well in soil that has bits of lava rock in it.

Hawaii's soil has bits of lava rock in it. Plants grow well in this soil.

Look around your neighborhood. What kinds of rocks can you find?

Studying rocks made by volcanoes is fun. Can you find rocks such as basalt, andesite, obsidian, or pumice where you live? Even if no volcanoes are in your area now, one might have been there millions of years ago. Be a volcano detective and see what you can find.

ON SHARING A BOOK

When you share a book with a child, you show that reading is important. To get the most out of the experience, read in a comfortable, quiet place. Turn off the television and limit other distractions, such as telephone calls. Be prepared to start slowly. Take turns reading parts of this book. Stop occasionally and discuss what you're reading. Talk about the photographs. If the child begins to lose interest, stop reading. When you pick up the book again, revisit the parts you have already read.

BE A VOCABULARY DETECTIVE

The word list on page 5 contains words that are important in understanding the topic of this book. Be word detectives and search for the words as you read the book together. Talk about what the words mean and how they are used in the sentence. Do any of these words have more than one meaning? You will find the words defined in a glossary on page 46.

WHAT ABOUT QUESTIONS?

Use questions to make sure the child understands the information in this book. Here are some suggestions:

> What did this paragraph tell us? What does this picture show? Where does magma come from? What are Earth's three layers? What do we call melted rock on Earth's surface? What is a crater? What are some kinds of rocks made by volcanoes? What is your favorite part of the book? Why?

If the child has questions, don't hesitate to respond with questions of your own, such as What do *you* think? Why? What is it that you don't know? If the child can't remember certain facts, turn to the index.

INTRODUCING THE INDEX

The index helps readers find information without searching through the whole book. Turn to the index on page 48. Choose an entry such as *rocks from volcanoes* and ask the child to use the index to find out why pumice rock floats. Repeat with as many entries as you like. Ask the child to point out the differences between an index and a glossary. (The index helps readers find information, while the glossary tells readers what words mean.)

LEARN MORE ABOUT
VOLCANOES

BOOKS
Cole, Joanna. *The Magic School Bus: Inside the Earth*. New York: Scholastic Press, 1997. Ms. Frizzle's class takes a field trip to Earth's center.

Green, Jen. *Mount Saint Helens*. Milwaukee: Gareth Stevens, 2005. Learn about the 1980 eruption of Mount Saint Helens in Washington State.

Nelson, Sharlene and Ted. *Hawaii Volcanoes National Park*. New York: Children's Press, 1998. Colorful photos and maps introduce readers to the national park that is home to two of the world's most active volcanoes.

Stamper, Judith. *Voyage to the Volcano*. New York: Scholastic, 2003. The Magic School Bus visits Hawaii's volcanoes.

WEBSITES
Stromboli Online—Volcano Expeditions
http://www.swisseduc.ch/stromboli/perm/index-en.html
See amazing photos of volcanoes from around the world.

Volcano Explorer: Virtual Volcano
http://kids.discovery.com/games/pompeii/pompeii.html
Build your own virtual volcano, then watch it erupt.

Volcano! Mountain of Fire
http://www.nationalgeographic.com/ngkids/0312/
This National Geographic Web page includes a volcano quiz.

Volcanoes
http://www.fema.gov/kids/volcano.htm
This website has volcano facts and information about how scientists study volcanoes.

GLOSSARY

ash: small rocks thrown out of volcanoes

caldera (kahl-DAIR-uh): a hole in the ground that forms when the rock above a magma chamber falls down

cinder (SIHN-duhr) cones: small volcanoes with very steep sides

composite (kahm-PAH-ziht) volcanoes: tall volcanoes with steep sides

crater: a hole in the ground that is shaped like a bowl

crust: Earth's outer layer. We live on Earth's crust.

erupts: spills out onto Earth's surface

hot spots: places in Earth's mantle that are hotter than the rest of the mantle

lahar (LAH-hahr): hot mud that flows quickly down the sides of a volcano

lava (LAH-vuh): melted rock on Earth's surface

magma (MAG-muh): melted rock that is inside Earth

magma chamber: an underground space that is filled with melted rock

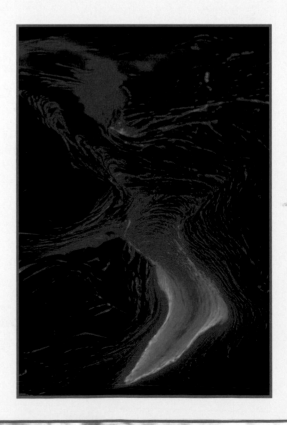

mantle: Earth's thick middle layer. The mantle is on top of the core and under the crust.

plates: huge pieces of rock that cover Earth's surface like the pieces of a puzzle

pyroclastic (PYE-roh-KLAS-tihk) rocks: rocks thrown out of a volcano

shield volcanoes: volcanoes whose sides are not steep

vent: an opening from which lava flows

volcanoes: places where hot, melted rock comes out of the ground

INDEX

Pages listed in **bold** type refer to photographs.